DISCOVER YOUR TALENT
and
FIND FULFILLMENT

A Guide to Using Your Skills to Get
What You Need and Want Out of Life

by
Roscoe Barnes III

Foreword by
Norman B. Rohrer

McKinley & Henson
P.O. Box 4382
Gettysburg, PA. 17325

DISCOVER YOUR TALENT and FIND FULFILLMENT: A Guide to Using Your Skills to Get What You Need and Want Out of Life by Roscoe Barnes III

Published by: McKinley & Henson
P.O. Box 4382
Gettysburg, PA 17325

Copyright © 1992 by Roscoe Barnes III

All rights reserved. No part of this book may be reproduced or transmitted in any form without written permission from the publisher, or author, except for brief quotations included in a review.

This book is sold with the understanding that neither the Author nor the Publisher is engaged in rendering legal, professional or financial services. Questions relevant to the practice of law, health or personal finance should be addressed to a member of those professions. The Author and Publisher specifically disclaim any liability, loss, or risk, personal or otherwise, which is incurred as a consequence, directly or indirectly, of the use and application of any of the contents of this work.

Cover Design created by Jan Pandolfino.

Printed in the United States of America
ISBN 0-9626420-0-2
Library of Congress Catalog Card Number 90-91628

ABOUT THE AUTHOR

ROSCOE BARNES III has established himself as a writer, artist, lecturer and minister.

AS A WRITER, he has worked as a news reporter for both military and civilian newspapers. In 1985, after working for The Enterprise-Tocsin, the Mississippi Press Association awarded him the First Place Award for Best Investigative Reporting. Since 1982, Barnes has published articles, book reviews, news stories and features in Inspirational, Military and Trade magazines. He has published fiction in literary magazines in the United States and in Germany.

AS AN ARTIST, Barnes has worked as an illustrator for The Nashville Graphic, an award-winning newspaper where he also provided editorial cartoons on local and national issues. His illustrations have also appeared in magazines and been commissioned by churches, businesses, individuals, military officials, and legal associations.

AS A SPEAKER, Barnes is in demand. For several years he hosted radio programs in several states. For the University of Maryland, he served as a Guest Lecturer and Writing Consultant for a Creative Writing course. For the National Bible Institute, he taught courses in Systematic Theology. After a successful inter-denominational preaching workshop in Germany, a U.S. Army Chaplain and Post Commander named a quarterly workshop in his honor: Barnes' Notes on Preaching, is the official title.

AS A MINISTER, Barnes has pastored churches since the early age of 17. He also served for seven years as a Chaplains Assistant in the U.S. Army.

Barnes, who has done graduate work with Boston University, holds a Master of Arts degree from the Lutheran Theological Seminary (Gettysburg, PA). He earned his B.S. and A.S. degrees (Cum Laude) from East Coast Bible College (Charlotte, N.C.). He is a graduate and member of the Christian Writers Guild (Hume, CA). Barnes is a native of Indianola, Mississippi.

DEDICATION

To Carla, the God-sent Poet who taught me much about life.
   My Sons: Roscoe IV, and Jeremy.
   My Daughters: Savannah, Toika, Crystal and Romesha.
   My Parents: Roscoe and Bertha Mae.
   My Brothers: Wiley, Roy Lee, Jimmy, Emerson and Lemuel.
   My Sisters: Alberta, Barbara, Vivian and Tina.
   My Teachers: Mr. Eddie Dennis, Mrs. Mary Kent,
      Coach Frank Brown and Mr. Carver Ransom.
   My Spiritual Mother: Mrs. Ellis of Pilgrim Rest Church of God.
   My Spiritual Starters: Anthony Williams, Bishop Willie Knighten,
      and Rev. Grey of Gentry High School.
   My MENTOR, TEACHER, FRIEND, IDOL, ROLE MODEL...the one and only person who inspired me and encouraged me as no other...the one who took me under his wings and nurtured me...the one who really believed in me from my youth...the one who convinced me to use my talents and be all that I could possibly be in life: Mr. Robert Whalen.
   My Dearest Friends: Marianne and Catherine Seavers, two wonderful, intelligent and multi-talented young ladies who have brought much fun and enjoyment in my life.
   My newest family, Debbie and Nate Sanders.

To all of these people I lovingly, respectfully, and happily dedicate this book.

TABLE OF CONTENTS

ABOUT THE AUTHOR
DEDICATION
ACKNOWLEDGMENTS
FOREWORD by Norman B. Rohrer
PREFACE: Why Another Book on Success and Fulfillment?
INTRODUCTION

Chapter 1
TALENT AND FULFILLMENT
Popular Misconceptions and Relevant Definitions......................11

Chapter 2
WASTED TALENT
A Growing Epidemic.....................17

Chapter 3
DISCOVER YOUR TALENT!
Proven Ways to Determine Your Gifts.....................23

Chapter 4
COMMON EXCUSES
Repeated Claims of Reluctant Achievers
and Realistic Responses.....................31

Chapter 5
PROVEN STEPS TO EXPLOIT YOUR TALENT
How to Get a Good Start.....................39

Chapter 6
OTHER STEPS TO USE YOUR TALENT
How to Have a Good Finish.....................49

Chapter 7
TALENT QUENCHERS
Seven Obstacles to Using Your Talent.....................57

Chapter 8
BLOOM WHERE YOU'RE PLANTED
How a Poor Man Found Riches.....................61

Chapter 9
THE SECOND WIND
Why You Should Keep Going When You Feel Like Quitting.....................63
AFTERWORD.....................67
RECOMMENDED SOURCES.....................68
THE TALENT RESOURCE GUIDE.....................70

ACKNOWLEDGMENTS

Scores of people have contributed to the writing and publication of this book. Information and help in one form or another have been contributed to this work by: Chaplain Chester and Rhoda Egert, Fr. Pat Connolly, O.P., Chaplain Myron S. Gerton, Jeff Wilson, Robert Wilridge, Baptist Baeumler, Dr. Jan Sutherland, Chaplain Reese Hutcheson, Chaplain John Hall, Chaplain Luke Pittman, Clinton Summerell, Lynn Durner, Tom and Marilyn Ross, Dan Poynter, Vernon Clay, Matthew Thomas, Anthony Gardner, Eric Piper, Elizabeth Gerton, Dr. George Voorhis, Dr. Kenneth Bell, Dr. Sammy Oxedine, Chaplain Andrew Bullard III, Rev. Caroll and Tammy Pusey, Wilmur Katie Clay, Shawn Birkotz, Sean Jenkins, Elder Gregory Howard, Elder Gerald Myers, Chanel Reeves, Jim Abbott, Michelle Carpenter, Hal Sharpe, Robert Holt, Traci Lower, Rev. Tyrone and Lareen Brown, Tony Hollins, Evang. Anthony Williams, Rev. Mark Walters, Calvin Griener, Prof. Norman Rohrer, Dr. Gerald Christianson, Dr. Nelson Strobert, Vicky Green, Chaplain Murel Beatty, Rev. Michael Cambell and Victor Mack.

Grateful acknowledgment is especially made to the following for permission to reprint previously published material: Excerpts: Reprinted by permission of Amistad Press Warner Books/New York from SUCCEEDING AGAINST THE ODDS, Copyright © 1989 by John H. Johnson & Lerone Bennett, Jr. Excerpts: HOW TO MAKE $2,000 A WEEK SELLING INFORMATION BY MAIL by Russ von Hoelscher, Profit Ideas, 254 E. Grand Ave., Escondido, CA 92025. Excerpts: Adapted and reprinted from STRAIGHT FROM THE HEART, copyright © 1987 Jesse L. Jackson, by permission of Augsburg Fortress.
Special thanks to Kristin Markle.

FOREWORD

Most beginning writers cleave to the illusion that all vocations require practice, hard work, and many hours of confining attention--except the one called writing. As a result, their manuscripts often miss the mark.

This book by a writer who has paid his dues is disillusioning to the amateur scribe. That's good-just the way it should be. <u>Discover Your Talent and Find Fulfillment</u> provides the proper orientation for people who have inspiring thoughts, discoveries, experiences, and insights to share through the printed page.

Roscoe Barnes guides the beginner through the editorial mine fields in this most appropriate and helpful format. He combines theory and actual examples, and there is no better combination for instruction. His book is basic editorial vanilla, presented with flair and clarity. His own editorial achievements have prepared him well for his role teacher and illustrator.

It is my prayer that this book will ignite in young adults a passion to discover and to efficiency use their God-given gifts. May they find realistic ways to enjoy their dreams.

Writing for periodicals is a good first step because it can lead to the more permanent type of writing as presented in books. Pay close attention to the author's personal experiences as a minister, writer, artist, speaker, and veteran of the U.S. military. He knows the guideposts on the path to success. Early writers who take heed will reach their goals.

I read hundreds of manuscripts every year prepared by beginning writers. I shall recommend this book as a first step toward success in feeding the hungry presses which are covering the world with blizzards of literature.

-- Norman B. Rohrer
Author and Director
Christian Writers Guild

PREFACE

WHY ANOTHER BOOK ON SUCCESS AND FULFILLMENT?

"The market is flooded with self-help books," a young man pointed out to me recently. "Particularly those on success and fulfillment. So why another one on the same subject?"

He posed a reasonable question. So I responded by pointing out the problems and weaknesses of the many existing books. I gave him the following list:

* Too many of the present books simply rehash other popular books on positive thinking and success-motivation.

* Many are too broad and scholarly for the average person.

* Many address the person who has already experienced some kind of success and financial blessing. These books appear to be aimed more toward those presently in the corporate structure.

* Many contain nothing more than get-rich-quick schemes that are overly optimistic or even false claims.

* Many are unrealistic in that they offer untried advice based on questionable theories instead of proven, practical experience.

* Many are so one-sided they encourage greed and selfishness. They promote an unhealthy desire for opulence.

* Many are written primarily to make money for the author, not to help the reader as they claim.

The young man to whom I was speaking nodded in agreement. He smiled and said, "Tell me, who is _this_ book for?"

"This book is for teen-agers, young adults, minorities, the unemployed, and those who are unsure about their future," I said. "It is for those who want the most out of life."

"Okay, that sounds good. So...how long is it?"

I smiled and said, "It's long enough to make the point, but short enough to tackle in one sitting."

Roscoe Barnes
February 1990

INTRODUCTION

This book is about Talent: What it is, how to find it and how to use it. I admit the market is flooded with books on success, money, and riches. There's a large number of books on positive thinking and entrepreneurship, not to mention magazines and a host of seminars. Some are good, some are not. On the religious side there's a gully-washer of stuff on health and healing-from both the Christian and the New Age perspective.

In light of this, I have struggled to be original, to say something new, something fresh. At the same time, I have tried not to compromise my own standards by promoting greed, materialism and false security. God forbid!

Life involves a tightrope, demanding a balance in all we do. It is hard to walk, but not impossible. In this material I have tried to show that fulfillment in life is not obtained by greed and arrogance. By the same token, it is not obtained by wimpiness and cowardice. There must be a balance.

Simply put, real success and fulfillment involve common sense, honesty and hard work. This focus is what sets my book apart from most others. It is realistic and practical in its approach. It offers no shortcuts. And while I believe in prosperity, I know that not everyone will become a millionaire. It is easier to discover their talents and find fulfillment, then let the wealth take care of itself.

Another element which sets this book apart from others is its focus on <u>raw talent</u> as the instrument for finding success, as opposed to mysticism, so-called psychic phenomena, and psychological gobbledygook.

I wrote this book with five objectives in mind. In nine chapters, I attempt to:
1. Explain how the development and use of one's talent can lead to a life of excellence and fulfillment.
2. Show how one may use proven principles to discover his or her talent.
3. Describe how one may use certain workable suggestions to get the maximum use of his or her talent.
4. Outline factors which may hinder the use of one's talent.
5. Illustrate how and why one may persevere in the use of his or her talent in the midst of discouraging circumstances.

The Bible says that a person's gift will make room for him or her and bring that person into the presence of kings and great people. That is my prayer and my dream for every reader of this book.

~CHAPTER ONE~
TALENT AND FULFILLMENT

What is talent? And what is the meaning of "fulfillment"? Ask ten people for a definition of "talent" or "fulfillment" and you will probably get ten different answers. To some, talent is something mysterious. It is something that only the "few and the proud" may have. And fulfillment? Many equate it with money, riches, a big home or a fine car.

All of these things may have their place, but my purpose here is to show how talent is something we're all born with and how the use of it may bring fulfillment, which may have little or nothing to do with getting rich. The basic premise for this work is the belief that every person has a purpose in life and that actual fulfillment can be experienced only after a person discovers that purpose. Even more, I hope to show that while it is crucial for a person to realize his or her talents, it is all too true that many talented people are not successful or fulfilled. "Nothing is more common than unsuccessful men with talent," said Calvin Coolidge, "unrewarded genius is almost a proverb."

TALENT AND SUCCESS

I used to think talent alone meant success, but I was wrong. The truth of this is quite convincing when you observe the people around you.

In his book, <u>Million Dollar Habits</u>, Robert J. Ringer says that it is important to understand that it's not what you have or what you do, but what you do with what you have. He went on to say that people often stumble or get trapped into careers without giving much thought to their talents, without even considering the possibility that they may be exploiting only a small percentage of their potential in their present job. Driving his point further, to show how it connects with fulfillment, Ringer said:

> Because it's so easy to miss your own talents, be sure to give this... a lot of attention and think objectively about your greatest strengths. The chances are overwhelming that efficient utilization of those strengths will also give you the most enjoyment, which in turn will save you from being obsessed with making money. The money will come, but you won't have to think about it; you'll be too busy enjoying your work and living in the present.

The bottom line is: No matter how talented a person might be, it profits nothing without efficient use.

FULFILLMENT AND FINANCES

I also used to think money was the ultimate source of happiness, and that if I had it, I would feel successful. What I found, however, was that fulfillment is not necessarily measured by dollars. Instead, it most likely is an individual thing that takes on a different meaning with each person. To a large degree it is satisfaction. It is being able to smile and say, "My living is not in vain!"

Life is replete with examples of people who had money without fulfillment. There are even those who forsook high-paying jobs and chose lesser-paying ones in search of fulfillment. Sometime ago, <u>USA Today</u> printed several articles about Nurses and Business people who left their professions to become teachers. They took huge pay-cuts. Yet, they felt it necessary in order to find fulfillment.

The other day I read of Arthur S. Harris Jr., a prominent writer who left the corporate world and started a career as a freelance writer. He acknowledged that he made more money as a corporate official but his career as a writer was "more fun than sitting in a corporate cubicle drafting a budget estimate."

A DEFINITION OF TALENT AND FULFILLMENT

Now in light of this, and in realizing how definitions may vary, you might ask: What exactly do you mean by Talent and Fulfillment? Good question. The answer, however, is elementary.

According to a Webster dictionary, fulfillment means, "to bring into actuality; to measure up, to be satisfied." And talent. according to <u>The Random House Dictionary,</u> is a "superior inborn capacity for a special field." "Inborn" is a good word. For talent is something a person brings from birth. Therefore, because of its innate characteristic, it is safe to assume that its discovery is a starting point for one to find success. I say "starting point" because the actuality of one's success is utimately depended upon the use of the talent discovered.

Dale Carnegie, author of the legendary, How to Win Friends and Influence People, echoed similar thoughts. In an ad with the headline: Why do some people achieve more than others? Carnegie Training officials said it would seem that when people are equal in intelligence, in desire and opportunity, they should be reasonably equal in achievement. But it doesn't work that way. Often one person will accomplish much more than another with about the same potential. The ad continued:

> It isn't the capacity that makes the difference. Virtually everyone has far more capacity than they will ever use. The real difference is that the achievers come to recognize their hidden resources and actively develop them in practical, useful skills and abilities which they can use every day for greater achievement. So it's what you do with what you have that makes the difference.

CLOSING THOUGHTS:

My proposal here is not a guarantee of riches. For no one can realistically make such a claim. But I do offer a promise of fulfillment. And when I submit that fulfillment is not always found in money, I speak not only from observation but from experience.

I once took a job in a factory warehouse. It paid well, and I worked until even my sweat was tired. The hours were long and the work was gruesome. The pay as good, but guess what? I lacked fulfillment. I had dollars but no delight. So I quit and became a news reporter at a local newspaper. The pay was less, but boy, was I fulfilled.

　　Now some people, I suppose, would call this insane. After all, we need money to pay bills. But the fact of the matter is, I found fulfillment--though not with riches. I had job satisfaction, a top priority for choosing a career, and I was thrilled beyond words. My enthusiasm led to creativity. This led to promotions. And this, not surprisingly, led to all the money I needed.

~CHAPTER TWO~

WASTED TALENT
A Growing Epidemic

It's been said the mind is a terrible thing to waste. I agree. But life taught me talent also is a terrible thing to waste. As I travel from year to year throughout the United States and abroad, I continue to meet people who are victims of wasted talent. These people are from all walks of life. And one thing (among others) I have found to be common about them is their treatment of achievers.

They either admire those who have reached the top, or they pool their resources to bring them down. Such actions remind me of the saying, "Misery loves company." I say this because the "have-nots" too often project a life which is bound by a bottom-rung mentality. They appear only to enjoy the company of the less fortunate. They get a kick out of being depressed and will readily exclude--and label--anyone who is positive. Not surprisingly, dreamers and doers are not welcomed in their company.

What a tragedy!

People all across the country are "sick" and crippled financially and socially. Young people are confused. Many suffer an inferiority complex. They don't know who they are, what they want or where they're going. You might say they are not "living," just merely existing. When I see this, I don't see a talent shortage. Instead, I see people who are bursting with potential. Some are loaded with several talents.

Yet, they have no solid future--or income--by means of it. And why?

It's because of wasted talent.

It's like a starving man who dies in a kitchen filled with food. He has the food, yet he dies because he refuses to eat what lies at his disposal. He doesn't use what he has. Likewise, people often are at the bottom because they fail to use what they have. Their talent is wasted. Such is not only bad for the individual, but wasted talent could be "fatal" to the economic structure of our communities. It is fatal to our status as role models, and it is fatal to our own self-worth.

"What is more tormenting than recognizing a potential and then refusing to put it to work?" asks Ted W. Engstrom in The Pursuit of Excellence. "It's like possessing a miracle drug capable of saving the lives of thousands but keeping it in a locked vault." Engstrom writes:

> The world's literature is filled with tales of men and women who knew their own potential, recognized their own talents but refused to use those gifts. Consequently, they are the truly tragic figures of history. It would be far better not to know of a gift than to be aware of it and refuse to use it.

Think of F. Scott Fitzgerald, the renown author of The Great Gatsby. He was a very prominent writer during the first half of this century and was envied by many. Yet, Ernest Hemingway is said to have criticized him sharply for wasting his talent by abusing the bottle. (Ernest, mind you, was no saint.)

SOME REASONS FOR WASTED TALENT

People with talent and gifts might fail to use them for any number of reasons. Following are some cases I've noticed along the way. (The names have been changed).

1. <u>Charlie is a good driver</u>. He has a high school education and can drive anything on wheels. He drives a public school bus part-time. He talks of being a model and of being a star. But all who know him say, "That boy was born to drive."

I talked to him about launching out and driving full-time. For several years I encouraged him to do this. But to this day he hasn't. His reason: "Man, I can't do that. I ain't smart enough."

Charlie's talent is being wasted because he feels <u>incompetent</u>. He's falling short because <u>he doesn't believe in himself</u>.

2. <u>David is a good writer</u>. He has pastored several churches and even taught a few high school courses. He writes plenty of poetry and heart-throbbing love letters to his wife. And his written sermons are well structured.

Having known him for over 12 years, I asked him about getting his work published. He wasn't interested, so I offered to help. Still he said he was not interested. Then after I continued "nagging" him about using his talent, he cried, "I'm no writer! It doesn't come easy. I have to sweat at it!"

David's talent is being wasted because of laziness. He can do it, but <u>he doesn't want to work hard</u>

to develop what he has.

3. <u>Johnny is an artist</u>. All through school he entered various art exhibits and contests. He won prizes and earned the respect of teachers and students. Today he is 25 and does nothing in the field of art. His reason: "I have to be in the mood for it."

Johnny's talent is wasted because of a <u>lack of discipline</u>. He has not learned that some things must be done as a matter of priority and not because of feelings.

4. <u>Wayne is a singer</u>. People everywhere compliment him on his voice. Whether in his room, in the shower, down the street, or on the job, he sings well. I noticed his talent and asked him why he wouldn't do something with it, such as performing in church or in some of the local clubs. After a while, he said, "I'd like to--but I don't know how to get started, or who I should contact."

Wayne's talent was wasted because of a <u>lack of knowledge</u> and <u>no contacts</u>.

5. <u>Lisa has a B.A. in Business Administration</u>. She lives in a small town that offers little or nothing in her field of study. In fact, most of the local businesses are small and very limited in what they could offer. Well, Lisa was offered several good jobs, but they were all out of state or at least a hundred miles away. So what did she do? She turned all of them down and chose to work in a local fish factory for minimum wages. She works incredibly hard--and long--for a little over three dollars an hour.

Lisa's business skills are being wasted because she's <u>afraid to leave home</u>.

6. <u>Robert is a dynamic leader</u>. He served in the

U.S. Army as a drill sergeant and holds a degree in business management. People I've met say Robert is a natural leader with raw talent. Until two years ago, he was respected by the entire community.

Robert is black. Because he was once mistreated and fired, he has become bitter, and somewhat paranoid. He now thinks all whites are racists, and he's convinced they are all out to get him.

This giant of a man has allowed <u>bitterness</u> to steal his future. Today, he is as prejudiced as those who mistreated him.

WHAT IS YOUR EXCUSE?

What are your reasons for not using your talent? Do you have any legitimate excuses? Perhaps you can identify with one of the cases above. Or maybe you know of someone who can.

"If a man has a talent and cannot use it," said Thomas Wolfe, "he has failed. If he has a talent and uses only half of it, he has partly failed. If he has a talent and learns somehow to use the whole of it, he has gloriously succeeded, and won a satisfaction and a triumph few men ever know."

What can you do that you are not ready to achieve?

~CHAPTER THREE~
DISCOVER YOUR TALENT!

It's been said that some of life's greatest problems can be solved with simple solutions. Some solutions, however, are so simple they are missed or ignored. For some reason, people find it hard to accept the <u>obvious</u> as being the <u>answer</u> to a tough problem. They feel that only the "secret" or the "mysterious" can serve as the solution in most cases.

The steps you are about to read are simple. In time you might find them profound. I have used them time and time again with astounding success. Take a look at these steps. Apply them and see what happens.

1. DETERMINE YOUR ASPIRATIONS

One of the first steps in discovering your talent is knowing what you desire. Often our talents and strengths lie in the things we enjoy. Perhaps Malcolm Forbes had this in mind when he offered "one meaningful definition" of success. He said it is doing what turns you on, and doing what you most want to be doing. In light of this, please take a moment to jot down all the things you like. Next, make a list of all the things you'd like to do. Then make a list of all the things you'd like to be. Keep this list before you and use it as a reference point to determine which goal is most important.

I believe God has given every person at least one

or more gifts. These gifts are skills, talents, aptitudes and potential to do certain things. Agreeing with this is Edith Schaeffer. In her book, <u>The Hidden Art of Homemaking</u>, she said, "Each person has...some talent which is unfufilled in some hidden area of his being, and which could be expressed and developed." Unfortunately, people often ignore (or never discover) their natural gifts. Then others who have realized their gifts never bother to develop them.

Needless to say, in most cases people tend to desire the things they're most capable of achieving. It seems their <u>aspirations match their natural gifts</u>.

My friend Chester is an example. From the time he was child, he enjoyed tearing things apart. He was curious about mechanical gadgets and how they worked. He carried a special interest in radios, watches and record players. He later dabbled with cars.

His family teased him. They called him "Doctor," and little did they know he would become a mechanical engineer.

Now that isn't strange. It was natural for him to enjoy what he did as a kid. It is natural for him to become an engineer. Why? Because that is his gift, his talent.

I encourage you to take note of your desires, your interests and your hobbies. Look at your dreams. The mere fact that you're interested in a certain thing could be evidence that you belong there and that you have raw talent in that particular area.

When I think of this subject, I'm reminded of something written by Bruce Lee, the great martial arts legend. He said, "It sometimes seems that intense desire creates not only its own opportunities, but its own talent as well."

Yes, desire--when reasonable--is a powerful force. It is also a guiding force. For under close scrutiny, it reveals a person's latent potential with which he or she was born. At the same time, it seems to create skills and opportunities a person never thought possible. Perhaps Stanislaus Leszcynski, King of Poland, was right when he said, "An earnest <u>desire</u> to succeed is almost always prognostic of success."

Take stock of your desires. They might be the map which will lead to a golden future.

2. DETERMINE YOUR STRONG POINTS

After you have determined what you'd like to do and what you'd like to be, your next step is to determine what you are good at doing.

Make a list.

Do you have a persuasive, convincing manner? Perhaps you'd make a good salesperson or a good lawyer. Are you good at giving advice? Then maybe you'd make a good counselor. Are you good with matching colors? Then perhaps you could choose commercial art, fashions, or interior decorating. The list could go on.

Now consider these questions:
1. Do you work better indoors or outdoors?
2. Do you work better alone or with a group?
3. Do you work better when giving orders or taking them?
4. Do you work better in one location or do you prefer traveling?

Answering these questions should help you to

pinpoint your interests. Similar questions are often given on aptitude tests to help people make wise career choices.

One of the most inspiring movies I've seen about choosing a career field is <u>Coal Miner's Daughter</u>. It is the story of Loretta Lynn, the "Queen of Country Music," and how she rose to stardom. I mention her because she is one of many, who without benefit of advanced education, discovered her talent--her place in life--by developing her strong points: singing and songwriting.

She received no special training in this field and for years, she didn't know she had it. But she kept singing around the kitchen, on the porch, and in the fields. Then her husband, who loved her singing, bought her a guitar. The rest is Country Music history.

She discovered her strong points and became "obsessed" with them. Some thanks are owed to her husband, who recognized her strengths and encouraged her. The fact that he played a role in helping her is what brings me to my next point.

3. LISTEN TO OTHERS

Listen to the advice and encouragement of those who know you and who recognize your strong points. Talk with them and consider their thoughts. Take note of all the compliments you receive. When several people praise you for a job well done, take stock in it. Start brainstorming and analyzing. Consider how that "job well done" might fit into your goals.

Consult with those who have succeeded in the field in which you are interested. Spend time with those who have interests or talents which are similar to yours.

If you'd like to be an auto mechanic, contact a local mechanic and get some advice. Chances are it won't even cost you. Tell this person of your interest and ask if you may pay him a visit. After you have made several contacts you will have more than enough information. This step will let you know if you've got what it takes. Also, it could possibly sharpen what you may already have.

I know of several men who've become established carpenters because as kids they followed their carpenter-dads. One man who'd been reared without a father obtained carpentry skills by bumping around with the father of his classmate. Today, this man from the single-parent home is manager of his own construction company.

I encourage you to listen and ask questions and you will learn and grow wiser.

4. DECIDE TO EXPERIMENT

There are some things you will never know until you ask-or try. This is what I say to people who are unsure about what talents they possess. Usually these people have interests in one or more areas. When I detect this, I ask if they've tried anything.

"No," many would say, "I couldn't do that, even if I wanted to!"

"But," I'd respond, "how do you know if you've never tried?"

Trying is the key. So experiment. Dare to do what you have desired. Never say you can't.

"But what if I fail?" you might ask.

Big deal. The "average" American millionaire has been bankrupt three times. You might fail several times, but even that is no proof that you're out of your league. Great people throughout history have tried and tried, only to fail and fail until they succeeded.

Think of Alex Haley, the Pulitzer prize-winning author of <u>Roots</u>. I read once that he wrote and struggled for eight years before he sold his first piece of writing. He received many rejection slips. He failed for many years to get something sold. But he kept trying and it paid off.

The same is true with me. I never knew I had talent to write until I gave it. There for about two years I experimented and took notes, treating myself as though I were a rat in a lab. I'd fail and try again. The rejection slips piled up. But I kept trying until I made it. (Many thanks to the Christian Writers Guild).

While growing up in a tiny southern town, I never dreamed of being a writer. But I tried it and after much effort discovered I had the talent to write. I later experimented and discovered I had talent for public speaking.

Again I stress: This is one of the primary ways of determining your gifts. Sometimes launching out into the unknown can be full of positive surprises. It can also reveal the areas in which you should not go. Experimenting can reveal your weak points and other qualities you might even despise. But again, you'll never know until you try.

Now pause for a moment. Think of all the things you'd like to do. Write them down. Now ask yourself if you've tried them. If not, make a separate list of the actions you will take in order to discover the talent you might or might not have.

What would you like to be? What would you like to do? Do you want to sing? Write? Be a photographer? A plumber? A preacher? A nurse? The sky is the limit. But all is dependent on your own inherent abilities and desires, and the resources you use in the process.

No matter what desire or desires you might have, the time is now to determine if you've got what it takes. Experiment!

TOO MANY TALENTS?

Have you ever met a person who was good at almost anything? Perhaps you know of someone who is good in about two or three different fields. I find that such people often consider themselves cursed. On one hand, you may feel cursed because you think you have no talents. On the other hand, you (or someone you know) may feel cursed because you are confused: you don't know which talent to use.

If you are a person with multiple talents and you are uncertain about what you should do, ask yourself:

1. Which of my gifts will provide for most of my needs?
2. Which of gifts should be used as a hobby?
3. Which of my gifts do I enjoy the most?
4. Which of my gifts will fulfill my ultimate dreams?
5. Which of my gifts (or how many) may I consolidate and bring into focus toward one goal?

A thoughtful response to these questions should

prove helpful, by allowing you to narrow your interests and bring your most important and necessary skills into focus, and into harmony with other responsibilities you might have.

I once approached a Catholic priest with my own "problem" of multiple talents. I could not decide what I should do. Then he told me of a friend who had several talents. This friend was a preacher, a writer, an artist, and a counselor. How did this guy handle his dilemma? He began writing articles and books using his own illustrations. Most of his writing consisted of material he'd preached and the things he'd gathered from counseling.

For the most part, this man felt he was a preacher. But he allowed his other talents to enhance and further his ministry. He found fulfillment with his many gifts by consolidating them and using them for his one main goal in life.

Your giftedness is a blessing from God. It is <u>not</u> a curse. Allow your gifts to complement each other in a way that will push you toward your number one goal.

~CHAPTER FOUR~
COMMOM EXCUSES FOR WASTED TALENT

Excuses are like hitchhikers. They try to hitch onto things in motion. They try extra hard to hitch onto people wanting to use their talent and onto people driving toward their dreams. Following are nine excuses which continue to thumb a ride along the Highway of Success. Look at them and see if they sound familiar. Then...keep on driving!

1. "I AIN'T SMART ENOUGH!"
If by "smart" you mean "educated", then your problem isn't as bad as it appears. We're living in a day when anyone can go to school, so take advantage of it. See an education/career counselor. Visit your library. Swing by a book store. Knowledge is all around, begging for a date with you.

2. "I DON'T HAVE THE MONEY."
When I speak of poverty, I can speak with conviction and much authority. For poverty was my bed-mate for many years. Nevertheless, I've learned that faith in God and faith in myself are the power twins that can put me over. In too many ways to mention, they, without fail, carved blessings out of the stones of my despair. I learned also that one must pool all of his or her resources, learn to save and manage finances.

Each day, more and more single parents struggle against the odds. They are crawling off welfare in order to find their dreams. These people have discovered education to be their beam of hope and they are marching toward it with dogged determination.

"Yes, it's hard," says Oprah Winfrey, "but it, (education), is the way out."

3. "I DON'T NEED COLLEGE!"

What a sad statement. Yet these words fall from the lips of both teenagers and adults. It seems incredible that anyone, in this age of advanced technology, would even think such a thing, let alone speak it.

A man once said to me, "I don't need school. I can get a job without it."

"Probably, but what kind of job?" I asked.

The person to whom I was speaking was in the U.S. Army. He'd been in for eight years and had not taken advantage of its educational benefits.

We paused in our conversation. Then I shared a classic illustration.

"You can chop down a tree with a dull axe or a sharp axe," I said. "But a sharp axe is better. A wise man would spend time sharpening his axe."

The man nodded as I continued. "It's the same with getting a job. To try for a job without education is like beating an oak tree with a dull axe. It might be possible, but it's foolish and a waste of time. It's best to educate yourself--sharpen your axe--and you may well get the job you need."

4. "WHAT IF I GET A DEGREE AND DON'T GET A JOB?"

This may happen, but consider these remarks by the Reverend Jesse Jackson:

"What we must do today is raise the expectation level of our people. Somebody says, 'Reverend, it's bad to raise their expectation, for if they excel and if their expectations are raised and opportunities are not there, they'll be frustrated.'

"But you can be frustrated with information, and you can be frustrated without information. The difference is that if you're frustrated without information, you can't do anything about it. But if you're frustrated with information, you can do something about it. So the odds are on your side. There's no guarantee that you won't be frustrated, but you increase the odds of survival.

"If people with a college degree can't get a job, when they get mad they can do something about it."

5. "YOU HAVE TO BE WHITE!"

If you buy into the thinking that only a certain race will make it in life you'll never experience your full potential. Frankly, I can think of no other phrase or thinking that has kept more people in bondage.

If you're surrounded by people who relish such negative talk, "Come out from among them and be ye separate!" Get inspired!

To suggest that one race is superior or smarter and the only race that will make it in life is a falsehood which can do unthinkable damage. As an antidote to such ignorance, consider Bill Cosby in entertainment, Michael Jackson in music, the Martin Luther King, Jr., Andrew Young and Jesse Jackson in politics, Johnson H. Johnson in publishing, Clarence Thomas in law, Alex Haley in writing, Tony Evans in the ministry, Oprah Winfrey and Bryant Gumbel with television news and talk show programs. The list could go on.

Listen to blacks and other minorities who've made it. Find a good role model, a good mentor and be motivated. Read their stories. Read their magazines. Read their books and "Go and do thou likewise!"

When people tell you only one race can prosper (whichever it might be), politely go out and prove them wrong. For real fulfillment in life is not determined by the color of one's skin, but by the content of one's character. "Nothing splendid has ever been achieved," said Bruce Barton, "except by those who dared believe that something inside them was superior to circumstance."

6. "SUCCESS IS ALL IN WHO YOU KNOW."

Really? Then be friendly and develop contacts. Be outgoing. Keep up with names. Send out cards, notes and letters on appropriate occasions.

While at work, do your best. Arrive early and leave late. Be honest and your boss (as well as others) will notice. They might even spread their compliments and and praise of you around the office, department, station, floor or even the community. As a result of such actions you will not only come to know people, but will be known by them as well.

Contrary to popular opinion, good news does travel!

7. "THERE ARE NO OPPORTUNITIES FOR MY TALENT."

If you feel opportunities or outlets don't exist for your talent, then take a bow. You now have the privilege of creating an opportunity.

No matter what your talent might be, your highest goal should be to excel. Let this be your passion--yes, even your life. "I've never sought success in order to get fame and money," said Ingrid Bergman, stressing, "It's the talent and the <u>passion</u> that count in success."

In your efforts to excel, you will learn that you can be so good that even your enemies will cut down high bushes to break down a path to your door. You can create a demand for your talent. But you must ignore mediocrity. Instead of worrying in the corner of frustrations, spend your time polishing, cultivating and developing yourself and your talent.

Worrying is a waste of time. It lacks the power to positively change even the smallest thing in your life. Therefore, I'd ask you not to wallow in it, as it can only darken your vision and make bad matters worse.

When you find yourself confused and feeling hopeless, try to snap out of it! Start brainstorming, maneuvering, praying, or whatever. Keep you head up and your face against the wind. You just might see your opportunity sooner than expected.

8. "AIN'T NO MONEY IN THIS FIELD!"

I hear this quite often from some of the most talented people around, particularly those in the field of art. About 90-95% of those I've met have never been paid for their talent. Most of these people choose to work in other fields, almost any field except the one wherein they're gifted.

What a tragedy, I thought. Then I realized their refusal to use their talent means open doors--and less competition--to those who'll not refuse.

I have also noticed that people will pay money for just about anything. Remember the pet rock? Modern Art?

9. "I DON'T HAVE TIME!"

Come on...stop fibbing! You have time to do what you really want to do. And if the time doesn't exist, you generally make the time. Right?

I have a friend who claims he wants to be a writer, but he says he doesn't have the time. Yet this same person can be seen spending several hours a day watching television and drinking beer. Well, to me it seems obvious that he's doing what he really wants to do--and it's not writing.

Alas!

I stress, therefore, that a person will make time to do the things he or she really wants to do. If a person truly wants to use his or her talents successfully, that person will sacrifice certain pleasures in order to do business. This could mean getting up early and sacrificing sleep. B.C. Forbes once noted that the great majority of conspicuously successful men are early risers. He opined: "To get up in the world, get up early in the morning."

Are you ambitious? "Much is not dared because

it seems hard," said Prince Anton von Kaunitz, an Austrian statesman. "Much seems hard only because it is not dared."

Well?

~CHAPTER FIVE~

PROVEN STEPS TO EXPLOIT YOUR TALENT
How to Get a Good Start

Discovering your talent is good. It's important. But learning to use what you've discovered is also important. It is a crucial part in your drive to find real fulfillment. Take a look at what follows. You'll find four practical points which you can began using today. Read them. Ponder them. Apply them, and see the difference they make in your life.

1. BECOME AN AVID READER

Reading is probably one of life's greatest tools of learning and yet one of the most neglected activities among those desiring personal fulfillment. I often say that if a person can read, he or she can do practically anything within reason because reading not only enables one to travel through time, across land and seas, but also allows one to learn and explore, to be enterprising and productive. "For one who reads, said Louis L'Amour, "there is no limit to the number lives that may be lived; for fiction, biography and history offer an inexhaustible number of lives in many parts of the world, in all periods of time."

Simply put, reading will enable a person to use the talent he or she is born to use.

This thought occurred to me while watching Steven, a young jack-of-all-trades. You see, Steven had no college degree. Yet he had a good job in at least three different fields. And because of his expertise, he netted an income which launched him far above the poverty level. Steven had spent many years on welfare, barely making ends meet. He was to some the epitome of "skid row." Then one day someone encouraged him to read about the things he'd like to do.

Previously, he bore a fierce appetite for comics, but his life was dramatically changed when he began reading nonfiction books, particularly, how-to books. He didn't have money to go to school, but he knew how to read. He couldn't afford to buy books so he visited his public library.

LEARNING ABOUT ANYTHING

There he was overwhelmed to find that he could learn almost anything by reading. "After all," he told me, "there is something written about nearly everything that's going on."

With these thoughts in mind Steven dove into books and magazines on plumbing. After practicing what he had read, he then read books on motivational success for self-encouragement. When he began to feel good about himself and his new-found knowledge, he then read books about job interviews and resumes.

Steven persisted in this reading habit for a couple of years. One day he hit pay-dirt and found total fulfillment.

He likes comparing himself with Abraham Lincoln. "Like ol' Abe, I'm a self-made...self-taught success story. I am what I am because of reading."

Steven is one of many who could attest to learning marketable skills as a result of reading. Be it books, magazines or newspapers, many a life has been changed.

On this note I would encourage you to subscribe for magazines and/or newsletters. Join a book club. Make the library your second home. In one sense, I'd say marry the library. Include the cost of books in your monthly budget. Set a goal to read a certain amount of material in your job field, talent field or simply your field of interest. See this as exercising and feeding the mind, and remember that as a result of these practices you can't get worse--only better!

Reading can reveal all sorts of channels and markets through which your talents can be used. Also, it can introduce you to key people with key information.

"One significant activity that distinguishes high achievers from their less successful counterparts," said George Gallup, Jr., "is their love of reading--and their corresponding lack of interest in television."

2. KEEP IN TOUCH

Keeping in touch with the people you know is a vital step to using your talent and tasting success. The word for this is Networking.

I realize that many people do not like writing letters, or sending cards each year to friends and relatives. Some figure it's too time-consuming. For the most part it might even seem worthless, but like it or not, keeping in touch has more value than many people realize. It pays, and it pays well.

Let me illustrate.

Tony spent four years in the U . S. Army. During that time he traveled throughout the U.S. and abroad. As a result, he met people and collected names and addresses at all of the places he visited. He soon had the names and addresses of over seven hundred people.

After he left the military, he'd send a card each year to every name.

Perhaps some would quickly argue that this is expensive, and in a sense it is. It does cost, but it also pays. And Tony soon discovered this when he started a mail-order business. He wanted to sell a certain product through direct mail and decided to use his seven hundred names.

Of the seven hundred people, about six hundred and fifty were ecstatic about his venture. They ordered his product and supplied him with the names of other potential buyers.

After selling his product for a year, Tony had a mailing list of three thousand names and the list is still growing.

Yes, it pays to keep in touch.

I used to criticize employers for hiring people they knew as opposed to those who were qualified but unknown. I blasted this practice until one day I realized: Even I would hire a friend or acquaintance over a stranger. This, I believe, is true with most people.

This is simply one more reason it pays to stay in touch with people. You never know when you might need them.

CARDS FOR SPECIAL OCCASIONS

I saw this advice in action as I worked with a number of business professionals. One guy in particular had a way of getting anything he wanted because he had friends--contacts. Because he sent out cards every year (during certain holidays), he was never forgotten by the people he'd call on for help.

I know of one lady (I'll call her Debra) who had at

least ten good friends in seven different states. She lost her job and began calling those friends, asking for assistance. Through their contacts Debra received nine good job opportunities in four different states.

This principle alone carries unlimited possibilities because everyone knows someone and is therefore able to recommend one person to another. "At all levels, from migrant farm workers to the top echelons of the business elite, some version of personal referral is the number one source of the job lead that results in employment, says Donald Asher, president of Resume Righters. Somehow the reality of this principle adds validity to the saying: It's not what you know, but who you know that counts.

3. ASK QUESTIONS

One thing I learned in grade school is that in order to get answers one must learn to ask questions. I also learned that a lot of people fail in life because they fail to ask questions. Perhaps it goes without saying thal we often "have not because we ask not."

It is good to be an avid reader to keep in touch with people. But a wise person will also be inquisitive about the job at hand. People of this caliber will ask questions of themselves and others. Such people will not settle for shallow or negative answers. Instead, they will drive themselves for answers that are concrete and full of substance and will not give up until such is accomplished.

Maybe it is safe to say: a person who is full of questions could easily become full of answers. Take my friend, Woody, for example. He observes everything. He carries a wealth of knowledge and can speak proficiently on just about any subject.

THE PRACTICE OF BEING "NOSY"

When I first met him, I thought he was a Harvard graduate. But I soon learned that he gained his knowledge by being "nosy." Woody is the type who would milk the brain of anyone he presumed to be smart. He'd question the mechanics at an auto shop until they were irritated. If he bought a screwdriver, he would beg the seller for all available information on screwdrivers. If he went to a funeral, he would inquire almost excessively of the directors about morbid experiences in their line of work.

Some thought his behavior was fanatical and immature. But educators, newsrooms and a string of employers thought he was the man for the job. He was in great demand. As far as I know, he still is in great demand. His questions brought hostility, but they also brought answers and information needed to put him on top.

Now, granted, you may not have to go as far as Woody to get answers, but you could emulate him to a degree and be flooded with profitable ideas.

4. BELIEVE IN YOURSELF

In order to garner the maximum use of your inborn skills, you must develop a sense of self-worth and self-potential. You have to believe in yourself, in your talents and in your dreams. Otherwise a sense of inadequacy will interfere with the attainment of your hopes.

Experience has shown me that the more I believe in myself, the more others will believe in me and respect me. And the less I believe in myself, the less others will believe in me.

Self-esteem, self-confidence and pride are three towers which stand out in most success books...and for good reason. For faith in yourself is a proven aid which can be the springboard to incredible achievements.

"Believe in yourself!" cries Norman Vincent Peale. "Have faith in your abilities! Without a humble but reasonable confidence in your own powers you cannot be successful or happy. But with self-confidence you can succeed."

There will always be some who will doubt your abilities, even after you've achieved some success. But you must prove them wrong, hold your head up and drive forward. Only then will you taste the rewards of your talent, the fruit of your labor.

This concept of believing in yourself involves other things. For one, it means daring to be yourself. Whether you're black, white, oriental, Jewish, Indian, or Hispanic, be proud of who you are. And never belittle yourself because of your background, race, or skin color. Instead, <u>convince yourself of the fact that you are as important as anyone</u>.

Strive to erase inferior thoughts and mediocre words from your mind and vocabulary. Think positively. Drive steadily and persistently for what you were born to do. Simply be yourself. There are enough carbon copies.

THE CHALLENGE OF BEING DIFFERENT

Be an original. After all, you are unique. You are an individual. There's only one of you. What's wrong with being different? Absolutely nothing! For there is at least one thing you can do like no other person.

When I began preaching as a teenager, I worried about how I should sound. I started by imitating other well-known, respectable preachers. As a result, I got minimal respect. Then one day I decided to be <u>myself</u>. When I did, I found other young preachers trying to imitate me.

Why not dare, right now, to be yourself, even if it means being different? Who knows? You might look around one day and see a crowd of admirers trying to imitate you.

There is much to be said about being different. Not infrequently, it is a primary reason for success. People tend to get tired of the old, the common and the familiar. That's why books are revised, products improved, and engines rebuilt. The world awaits the new, the fresh, the innovative. I am always amazed at singer Michael Jackson and how he initiates various fads, such as the white glove on one hand and tape around his fingers.

Michael, like other achievers, consistently dares to be different. After all, he's doing what he likes because he's <u>being</u> himself. And he's being himself, presumably, because he <u>believes</u> in himself.

<u>CLOSING THOUGHTS</u>

Your quest for real fulfillment may not carry you on Easy Street. Yet, because of your inborn, God-given gifts, you may capture your dream and find authentic happiness on Any Street, despite the herd of obstacles you will face.

I offer the four points in this chapter as starters.

They should be used, therefore, as preparatory tools to get your ready for stepping out to use your talents. In the next chapter, I will give four other points which should help you to continue toward your goal and on to having a nice finish.

~CHAPTER SIX~

OTHER STEPS TO USE YOUR TALENT
How to Have a Good Finish

In the previous chapter I focused on ways to get a good start in the use of your talent. In this section I will show you four things you must do to continue making use of your talent and what you must do to have a good finish.

What you will find are factors you've probably heard before. Most likely, things that "Mama taught us." Nevertheless, if by reading this you gain new insight (because of the perspective I have chosen), I will be grateful. As I mentioned earlier, I have tried to say some old things in a fresh, more practical and encouraging way. After all, nothing is new under the sun.

Don't be surprise then, if when you are done, you say: All that I needed to know about using my talent I learned from Mama.

Well, let's dive in.

1. WORK HARD FOR THINGS YOU NEED AND WANT

The first point of this chapter should come as no surprise. For nothing will take the place of hard work.

"History, money, and all the forces of the universe are on the side of the man or woman who sets a goal and works night and day to achieve it," said John H. Johnson in <u>Succeeding Against the Odds</u>. "That person may not win what he wants to win--which may not be, in the long sight of history, what he or she needs to win--but if he continues to work and will, he can't be denied."

This principle is vital to any ambitious person and it is a truth that my father instilled in me at an early age. There's nothing magical or miraculous about it. It's just a plain and simple fact that good things come to those who not only wait, but work.

If you show me a lazy man, I'll show you a "dying" man. I can say this because action and creativity are signs of life, and a person lacking such qualities may not be around very long, particularly in the world of achievement. You see, achievers and talent-users are people who take action. They set things in motion because they're in motion. They're bothered with few distractions because, like a rolling stone, they don't stop to gather moss. Russ Von Hoelscher, a mail-order giant, put it this way: "There is power in taking action. Although I believe in the benefits of meditation, I think most of us need to spend only 5% of our time thinking, planning and meditating, and 95 of our time taking positive action."

Hoelscher went on to say that if a person has decided to do a certain thing, there comes a time to "stop thinking about it, stop talking about it--do it!"

"Nothing comes easy," says Norman Rohrer, author and director of the Christian Writers Guild. "If you want to succeed...you have to pay a price."

Norman was speaking of success as a writer, but the principle of hard work and "grinding at the mill" applies to other areas as well. Norman teaches that one must be willing to pay his dues if he wants to use his talent and achieve some kind of success.

No matter what your talent or goals might be, never shun hard work. Learn to sweat, maneuver, negotiate, plead, beg, scream, shout, and pray until your goals are met.

"Hard work ain't never killed nobody!" my father used to say. And then he'd prove it by providing for our family. He taught me hard work is a bridge by which one reaches his place in life.

My mother agreed. "Don't be afraid of hard work," she'd say. "It won't kill you, but laziness will!"

Need I say more?

2. BE HONEST IN ALL YOUR DEALINGS

Honesty is the best policy.

This time honored phrase may be trite but it is true. You've heard it before. Perhaps you've heard it a hundred times. I want to repeat it with a slight alteration: Honesty still is the best policy.

"No dream is worth the cost of dishonesty," says Charles R. Swindoll. In his book Make Your Dream Come True, he said, "Any illegal or less-than-honest shortcut to success will carry a high price tag--for you or for someone else. The only answer to that cost, simplistic though it may seem, is a return to honesty. Integrity may be an even better word."

When I think on this subject I'm reminded of two verses of Scripture:

1. "Therefore all things whatsoever ye would that men should do to you, do ye even so to them." (Matthew 7:12)

2. "...For whatsoever a man soweth, that shall he also reap." (Galatians 6:7)

Over the years I've spoken with many people who

disagreed with the honesty policy. In fact, they considered it a "wimpy philosophy." They bought the adage, "All is fair in love and war."

Unfortunately, I should mention that few of these people are truly fulfilled in life. Most of them are either in prison, sick, or flat broke. Some suffer from guilt, and still others have problems with insomnia, while some go to broken homes, drugs and alcohol.

You see, there's a terrible price to being dishonest. Of course this may sound elementary, but one fact remains: you won't go wrong in obeying the laws of the land. Stick with the golden rule by treating others the way you'd want to be treated. Then you may appreciate that timeless axiom by Thomas Dekker, which says, "Honest labour bears a lovely face."

3. HELP OTHERS AS MUCH AND AS OFTEN AS YOU CAN

In addition to working hard and being honest, you can joyfully use your talent--and continue to do so--if you consider the needs of others.

Reaching down and helping someone in need is a mighty step toward excellence. It is not only a means by which you can have satisfaction, it's also to some degree an investment. And it happens to be an investment with guaranteed returns.

Ralph Waldo Emerson said, "It's one of the most beautiful compensations of life that no man can sincerely try to help another without helping himself."

On a related note, Christ said, "Give, and it shall be given unto you; good measure, pressed down, and shaken together, and running over, shall men give into your bosom. For with the same measure that ye mete withal it shall be measured to you again." (Luke 6:38)

By helping others we help ourselves. By promoting others we promote ourselves. I think it's justifiable to say that <u>we'll rise only as high as we strive to raise others</u>. For our altitude in life will be determined by our <u>attitude</u> towards others.

A SOLDIER'S STORY

Near the close of World War II, a soldier who was almost frozen became lost in a snow-covered wooded area in Germany. He'd wandered for miles and days without finding his men. Therefore, overwhelmed with despondency he decided to give up and die in the snow. He sat on what appeared to be a snow-covered log. He had been sitting for three minutes when the "log" shifted. The soldier jumped. He heard a sound, a grunt, a moan.

He discovered his "log" to be another man who'd given up and was nearly frozen to death. Immediately the tired soldier brushed the snow and ice from the man and proceeded to warm him, administering first-aid.

The soldier became so involved with helping the dying man that he forgot his own problem. As a result, they both survived.

The first soldier kept his own blood flowing as he sought to do the same for another. He kept his own limbs in motion as he sought to do the same for another.

And so it is with life. It's the same with jobs, careers and relationships. Much of it has to do not only with action but with attitude as well.

Speaking along this same line, Jesse Jackson

once said, "Never look down on anybody unless you're helping him up."

Quite a mouthful, huh? Well, if you desire to use your abilities, if you wish to find fulfillment, if you long to find employment and be financially secure, I challenge you to help others. Don't wait on the less-fortunate to come knocking on your door. Rather, seek them out. Save them. Rescue the perishing!

Throw out a lifeline! <u>Use your talent for the good of others as well as yourself</u> and you will be set on the path to genuine satisfaction.

4. STAY FIT

Why is it that some jobs require applicants to be examined before beginning work? Why does the military require the same? Is it not to make sure that the people interested and applying are fit for the tasks?

It goes without saying that a good, strong body and sound mind will help to produce good, strong, quality work. Since the early '70's, more and more Americans have discovered this truth and have started getting in shape by establishing some kind of daily exercise program. As a result, they feel better, they work better, they think better, they look better and they live longer.

This advice to get in shape (and stay in shape) cannot be over emphasized. Not only can it be a matter of success and failure as far as your talent and goals are concerned, it can literally be a matter of life and death.

Not a few talented and successful people have shortened their careers by an early death because of poor eating habits and lack of exercise.

Therefore, I encourage you to see a doctor and take part in some kind of fitness program. This you'll never regret. Also remember the old proverb: "An ounce of prevention is better than a pound cure."

CLOSING THOUGHTS

As I bring this chapter to a close, let me remind you that only a deliberate effort on your part will cause your goals and dreams to materialize. Whether you aspire to be an author of books, "a writer of songs, or someone involved in other aspects of creative art, the rewards inherent in these endeavors don't happen just by chance," says Melvin Powers, publisher of Wilshire Book Company. "You have to make them happen. You must plan for them with as much care and deliberation as you would to structure a building."

Short-cuts do not exist here. But don't lose heart. God has gifted you and He has a plan and purpose for your life. Let the discovery of His will bring you the joy you've always wanted.

AN OVERVIEW

Remember that in order to get a good start in using your talent, strive to:
 1. Become an avid reader.
 2. Keep in touch with people you know.
 3. Ask questions of yourself and others.
 4. Believe in yourself.

To continue the use of your talent and have a good finish, remember to:
 1. Work hard for the things you need and want.
 2. Be honest in all your dealings.

3. Help others as much and as often as you can.
4. Stay fit.

~CHAPTER SEVEN~
TALENT QUENCHERS

Still serious about using your talent to find fulfillment? Then drive on...but be on the lookout for the "Talent Quenchers." I've listed seven of them to avoid at all cost.

Be alert and on guard for the following:

1. PROCRASTINATION

The procrastination business is a mighty tiresome facet of life, says Wayne W. Dyer, author of <u>Your Erroneous Zones</u>. "If you've got a bad case," he adds, "hardly a day goes by that you don't say, 'I know I should be doing it, but I'll get around to it later.'"

Dyer suggests that this universal enigma is an expression of self-doubt, self-delusion, and a way of giving in to escapism, which may lead, inevitably, to boredom. He notes, however, that "by doing what you choose, now, or using your mind in creative new ways now, you can insure that you'll never again choose boredom for yourself. The choice, as always, is yours."

2. LAZINESS

"Lazy hands make a man poor, but diligent hands bring wealth" Proverbs 10:4 (NIV).

In a letter to Winston Churchill, Jennie Jerome Churchill wrote: "You seem to have no real purpose in life and won't realize at the age of twenty-two that for a man life means work, and hard work if you mean to succeed. "

How true! And would it not also be fitting--and most helpful--to remember the line from Smollett: "The victory of success is half won when one gains the habit of work."

3. SHORTCUTS

Never waste your time looking for an easy way to success. If something seems too good to be true, says the age-old proverb, it probably is. Looking for shortcuts often means getting ripped off. "There is no <u>way</u> to succeed and have the lovely spoils-money, recognition, <u>deep</u> satisfaction in your work," said Helen Gurley Brown, "except to put in the hours, (and) do the drudgery." This whole idea about avoiding shortcuts has been proposed by numerous experts, counselors, and leaders, including Ann Landers.

4. BITTERNESS

Oppose bitterness with all you've got. Few things can cause more self-destruction. There is never a legitimate reason to be bitter, any more than there is a legitimate reason to commit suicide.

Just before her execution in 1915, Edith Cavell said, "Standing, as I do, in the view of God and eternity I realize that patriotism is not enough. I must have no <u>hatred</u> or <u>bitterness</u> towards anyone."

Is this not a healthy view on the place of bitterness?

5. JEALOUSY

Another sure way to misery and disaster is the seemingly compulsive habit to keep up with the Joneses. In practically all the places I have visited I have met people who were up to their necks in debt. It was all because of jealousy. They felt that life wasn't life unless they could out-do their neighbors. "O! beware, my lord, of jealousy," wrote Shakespeare in Othello. "It is the green-ey'd monster which doth mock the meat it feeds on."

6. ARROGANCE

Feeling you are above others and stepping on them to reach the top is a definite no-no.

"When pride comes, then comes disgrace, but with humility comes wisdom" (Proverbs 11:2, NIV).

7. GREED

When faced with this quencher, remember the man with the goose that laid golden eggs.

"Money, fame and power, as intentions, are deadly," say John-Roger and Peter McWilliams, authors of <u>Do It!</u>. "People pursue them, get them, are not happy (in fact, are usually more unhappy). Then they decide, 'It must not be <u>enough</u>. I need more, <u>then</u> I'll be happy.' So they set their sights higher, get more of the thing that didn't make them happy in the first place, and are unhappier still.

"As with any addictive substance, by now they're hooked. Life becomes the relentless pursuit of more! More! More!"

~CHAPTER EIGHT~
BLOOM WHERE YOU'RE PLANTED!
How a Poor Man Found Riches

"Stop griping where you've grown and start blooming where you're planted."

This advice, where appropriate, has made people rich and famous. Even more, it has brought many to a state of fulfillment. One such person who comes to mind is John H. Johnson. Over forty years ago he borrowed $500 on his mother's furniture and created a business empire.

He began work at Supreme Liberty Life Insurance Company, and was considered the low man in the company's power structure. While there was much room for griping, he made the best of a bad situation. Here's what he said:

"...There are so many twists and turns in a life that you never know where a job, however small, will lead you. It's in your interest...to do every task assigned you well, for you never know where these skills can be utilized later."

Today he is considered one of the 400 richest men in America. Despite his many obstacles, he rose from the welfare rolls of the Depression to become the most successful black businessman in America's history. He is the founder of Ebony, Jet, and EM magazines.

Have you desired to find a better job? Start a business? How many times were you turned down? Perhaps your friends, relatives and even banks have discouraged you. If this is the case, consider what follows.

Before Johnson started his first publication, he needed to have a good financial base. He went to a bank in Chicago which turned him down because he was "colored." He went from office to office and "was told no and hell, no!"

Even a trusted friend told him, "Save your money, young man. Save your energy. Save yourself a lot of disappointment."

How would you respond to these remarks? Would they shatter your dreams and melt your vision?

Many times it's not the rejection that ruins our hopes and shatters our dreams. Rather it's how we respond to rejection. Johnson said that when he was told, "Boy, we don't make any loans to colored people," he felt a flash of anger. But instead of getting mad, he got smart. As a result, he discovered another source.

Perhaps your frustrations for being rejected are legitimate. But believe it or not, if you respond negatively, you're shooting yourself in the foot. You are adding to your obstacles and making it harder to rebound. Johnson had talent and a dream, and he was determined to carry it through to fruition. Yes, he made it. He reached his goals. He bloomed where he was planted.

When I think of Johnson's accomplishments, I have to agree with Booker T. Washington: "Success is to be measured not so much by the position that one has reached in life as by the obstacle which one has overcome while trying to succeed."

~CHAPTER NINE~
THE SECOND WIND
Why You Should Keep Going When You Feel Like Quitting

To achieve a goal by means of your talent might require going for the "second wind." I learned this in Basic Training. I had run three and one half miles and was nearing the fourth mile when I felt a sudden burst of pain in my chest. My legs screamed in agony and my head pounded furiously.

I wanted to quit. My body wanted to quit. But my Drill Instructor shouted, "The second wind! Go for the second wind!"

<u>What's the second wind</u>? I asked myself. <u>Besides, who cares</u>?

About five minutes later, from somewhere I felt a burst of energy. My lungs expanded and my strength revived.

I can make it! I told myself. I can make it!

When I felt I could go no further I reached my second wind which carried me another three miles.

Too often ambitious people with dreams and talent fall short--even flat on their faces--because they give up too soon. One of the keys to success and fulfillment, stressed by most success books, is determination. A person needs determination to succeed in anything. Sometimes you have to grit your teeth, clench your fists and refuse to give up. You must be fixed until your dream is a tangible reality.

You have to go and keep going, despite the odds. And if you persist, you'll catch your "second wind." Your endurance will pay off and open doors beyond your dreams.

Let's face it. Fulfillment in many cases has been lost because the person in search of it stopped too soon to experience it. "Nothing in the world can take the place of persistence," Calvin Coolidge said. ""Talent will not. Genius will not. Education will not. Persistence and determination alone are omnipotent!"

When was the last time you felt discouraged? How long did you fight? Did you give up after the first battle? Did you try again? Or did you go until you could see a difference.

A story is told of an ambitious gold prospector who went out west during the renowned Gold Rush in California. The digger, who'd been a poor farmer most of his life, found a place and commenced to digging. He dug for days, he dug for weeks and he dug for months, but found no gold. So he gave up. After five and one half months of digging, he convinced himself that no gold was in his area of work.

He packed up and left, boiling with frustration. Shortly after he left, a young Indian man took his place. The Indian dug for only three hours, and guess what? You're right. He hit solid gold!

Now think about it. Three hours! If the farmer had endured for three more hours his life would've been changed forever. He was so close, yet so far from his dream because he gave up.

In all of our struggles we should remember that our goals are often closer than we realize.

Now pause for a moment and reflect on your past

endeavors. Did you quit school because you thought you couldn't make it? Did you quit a job because you didn't think you could handle the pressure? Have you quit anything because you felt you could not be all you wanted to be?

Most likely you answered "yes" to at least one of the above questions. If you did then take a moment to think of what could've happened if you'd stayed. Did the situation appear to be getting better soon after you left? Did the people involved appear to be different? As you look back, do you have any regrets? Possibly if you'd stayed you might have made a difference.

Agree?

Well, so much for the past. You can't change that. But you can have some control over your present and future. Decide here and now, from this point on, you will not crumble under obstacles. Instead, you will fight until a change is seen. It doesn't matter how big or how small the change might be, simply determine you will stick to your dream until it becomes a reality.

If you feel depressed and discouraged, keep on running. Keep on sweating. You are today closer to your goal than you were yesterday. Every step counts. So keep on "digging." You might be much closer to your goal than you realize.

"I hold a doctrine to which I owe much, indeed, but all the little I ever had," said T. F. Buxton, "namely, that with ordinary talent and extraordinary perserverance, all things are attainable."

~AFTERWORD~

I wrote <u>Discover Your Talent and Find Fulfillment</u> out a sincere desire to help people discover their God-given gifts and find practical ways to use their gifts to attain excellence and lasting satisfaction. I aimed to write a concise, informative and workable guide that would be easy to read and fun to follow. Also, I'd hoped to ignite in people a <u>passion</u> to put their talents to work.

Of course, no one book can answer all questions or address all issues. Therefore, future revisions of <u>Discover Your Talent</u> are in store. You can help me improve future editions (and other books) by offering your suggestions. Please answer the following questions by mail.

1. Did you enjoy reading this book? Why?
2. What idea in the book impressed you the most?
3. What other questions or problems do you have which are not addressed in this book?

Although I can't guarantee success, the principles offered here are tried and proven. Let me hear from you. I would be happy to help you in any way possible.

In the meantime, I wish you the best of excellence and pray that your gifts will open exciting doors of opportunity for you and your beloveds!

~RECOMMENDED SOURCES~

BOOKS TO HELP YOU ASSESS YOUR TALENT:

What Color is Your Parachute: A Practical Manual for Job Hunters and Career Changers, by Richard Nelson Bolles, Ten Speed Press, Box 7123, Berkeley, CA 94707

Test Yourself - Find Your Hidden Talent, by Jack Shafer, Wilshire Book Company, 12015 Sherman Rd., North Hollywood, CA 91605

Discover What You're Best At, by Barry and Linda Gale, Simon & Schuster, 1230 Ave. of the Americas, New York, NY 10020

The Hidden Art of Homemaking, by Edith Schaeffer, Tyndale House Publishers, Inc., Wheaton, IL 60189

COURSES AND SCHOOLS TO HELP YOU SHARPEN YOUR TALENT:

Discover Your Possibilities in Writing, by Norman B. Rohrer, The Christian Writers Guild, 260 Fern Lake, Hume, CA 93628

ICS- International Correspondence Schools, Scranton, PA 18515

North Light Art School, 1507 Dana Ave., Cincinnati, OH 45207

Art Instruction Schools, 500 S. 4th St., Minneapolis, MN 55415

BOOKS TO HELP YOU FIND AND MAINTAIN MOTIVATION:

Succeeding Against the Odds, by John H. Johnson with Lerone Bennett, Jr., Warner Books, 666 Fifth Ave., New York, NY 10103

Live Your Dreams, by Les Brown, William Morrow, 105 Madison Ave., New York, NY 10016

Education of a Wandering Man, by Louis L'Amour, Bantam Books, 666 Fifth Ave., New York, NY 10103

The Pursuit of Excellence, by Ted W. Engstrom, Zondervan, 1415 Lake Dr., S.E., Grand Rapids, MI 49506

Do It! Let's Get Off Our Buts, by John-Roger and Peter McWilliams, Prelude Press, 8165 Mannix Dr., Los Angeles, CA 90046

Straight from the Heart, by the Rev. Jesse Jackson, Fortress Press, Philadelphia, PA

Million Dollar Habits, by Robert J. Ringer, Fawcett Crest, New York, NY

Stay Home and Make Money, by Russ von Hoelscher, Profit Ideas, 8361 Vickers, Suite 304, San Diego, CA 92111

Books that Made the Difference: What People Told Us, by Gordon and Patricia Sabine, The Shoe String Press, Inc., Hamden, CT 06514

THE TALENT RESOURCE GUIDE

Use this Talent Resource Guide when you really want to develop and efficiently use your natural gifts. Examine closely. You'll find--right here--the tools you need to become a success in business, writing, art, speech, school, management, and many other fields.

Whether you need instruction or motivation, YOU NEED THE RESOURCES IN THIS GUIDE! Order directly from: McKinley & Henson, P.O. Box 4382, Gettysburg, PA 17325.

....

BUSINESS

B1 - BUSINESS BUILDING IDEAS FOR FRANCHISES AND SMALL BUSINESS
by Med Serif

One of the most important operations in any business is a well-planned and executed promotion program. It must be important--it brings in the customers. By successfully implementing only one of the ideas presented you can earn the cost of the book a thousand times over.
--Only $3.95

B2 - A WOMAN'S GUIDE TO STARTING A SMALL BUSINESS
by Mary Lester

Shows what other women have accomplished by starting imaginative ventures and points out the many possibilities open to you. Covers low-overhead businesses, evaluating your potential and finding business management assistance. --Only $3.95

B3 - HOW TO TURN YOUR IDEAS INTO DOLLARS
by Gary Null and R. Simonson

You may be sitting on top of a fortune and not realize it. This book provides you with a step-by-step formula for creating profitable ideas and then shows you how to market them. --Only $3.95

B4 - THE GARAGE SALE HANDBOOK
    by Peggy Hitchcock
Shows you how to use a business-like approach to holding a garage sale (also known as a patio, yard, porch, basement, barn or attic sale) and make large profits.   --Only $3.95

B5 - THE UNABASHED SELF-PROMOTER'S GUIDE: What Every Man, Woman, Child and Organization in America Needs To Know About Getting Ahead by Exploiting The Media
    by Jeffrey Lant, Ph.D.
If you buy only one book to promote your talent, make sure you get this one! It provides everything you need to know to promote your service, product, cause or organization through every kind of free media. It's the best!   --Only $35.95

B6 - MAKING MONEY FOR YOURSELF
    by Russ von Hoelscher and George Sterne
This is the No.1 source of information on how to start your own business. Learn how to discover the right business opportunity for you and get started from scratch, or buy an existing business at the lowest possible price and/or the very best terms.   --Only $14.95

B7 - STAY HOME AND MAKE MONEY
    by Russ von Hoelscher
This the leading source guide for today's best home business opportunites. Full time or spare time, you start making big profits in the safety and comfort of your own home. This exciting new book presents you with scores of new, proven, profitable ways to have your cake and eat it, too, as the happy owner of a moneymaking home-based business.   --Only $14.95

B8 - MONEY MAKING MARKETING: Finding The People Who Need What You're Selling And Making Sure They Buy It
    by Jeffrey Lant, Ph.D.
You'll never play guessing games again with your marketing efforts after reading this revealing book. It shows you how to create a marketing system that sells more of your talent, product/services every

single day!   --Only $35.00

B9 - <u>NO MORE COLD CALLS</u>: The Complete Guide to Generating--And Closing--All the Prospects You Need To Become A Multi-Millionaire By Selling Your Service
    by Jeffrey Lant, Ph.D.
If you're running a service business--any service business--and aren't yet making the money you need, this book was written especially for you! Are you a doctor, lawyer, dietitian, consultant, engineer, tinker, tailor, private investigator, dog walker, house sitter, landscape architect, barber, caterer...or any one of millions of other service providers who hasn't yet turned your service business into a certain means of making yourself rich? Then this giant 680-page resource has just what you need.   --Only $44.95

B10 - <u>REAL ESTATE WEALTH BUILDING OPPORTUNITIES</u>
    by Russ von Hoelscher
Real estate has created more millionaires than all other wealth-building systems combined. This big 310-page manual gives you a dynamic shortcut strategy that can lead you to fabulous riches. Here's everything you need to know to win when you buy or sell real estate--all in plain English. Includes a unique master plan on how to pyramid a measly one thousand dollar investment into one million dollars.   --Only $14.95

ADVERTISING

A1 - <u>$50,000 A YEAR FROM MAIL ORDER ADVERTISING</u>
    by Lee Howard
Use this manual to learn how to write successful advertising copy. From A to Z in content, composition, attention devices, placement. It's all here.   --Only $12.00

A2 - <u>CASH COPY</u>: How To Offer Your Products And Services So Your Prospects Buy Them...NOW!
    by Jeffrey Lant, Ph.D.
This big 480-page book tells you how to turn every marketing communication you ever write into one that makes you money. Now!
    --Only $30.00

A3 - <u>HOW TO WRITE A GOOD ADVERTISEMENT</u>: A Short Course In Copywriting
    by Vic Schwab

A must book for any prospective advertiser or direct mail operator. 220 pages of understandable, applicable, copywriting gospel.
    --Only $20.00

CONSULTING

C1 - <u>THE CONSULTANT'S KIT</u>: Establishing And Operating Your Own Successful Consulting Business
    by Jeffrey Lant, Ph.D.

This is the only book specifically recommended by the U.S. Small Business Administration for new and aspiring consultants in any field. Thousands of people nationwide are now profiting from the precise steps in this 203 page book.   --Only $35.00

C2 - <u>HOW TO MAKE AT LEAST $100,000 EVERY YEAR AS A SUCCESSFUL CONSULTANT IN YOUR OWN FIELD</u>: The Complete Guide to Succeeding In The Advice Business
    by Jeffrey Lant, Ph.D.

This 315-page book takes up where THE CONSULTANT'S KIT leaves off. If you have problem-solving information at your disposal and want to profit from it, use the book that expert after expert agrees is breathtakingly complete. Never give anyone a piece of your mind again. Now sell it to them for what your information is really worth.
    --Only $35.00

PUBLIC SPEAKING & SEMINARS/WORKSHOPS

S1 - <u>ORGANIZING AND OPERATING PROFITABLE WORKSHOP CLASSES</u>
    by Janet Ruhe-Schoen

Covers where to set up classes, developing the curriculum, what to charge, how to sign up students, and how to promote your workshop in your community. If you know and enjoy your subject, you can organize and teach workshop classes. --Only $3.95

S2- PREPARING EFFECTIVE PRESENTATIONS
by Ray J. Friant, Jr.
How to develop presentations that pay off. The book shows that the preparation of an effective presentation is not complicated, difficult or time consuming. The material covered is stripped of time consuming and wasteful verbiage and offers a simple methodology for presenting complicated ideas to diverse audiences.
--Only $3.95

S3 - HOW TO HANDLE SPEECHWRITING ASSIGNMENTS
by Douglas P. Starr
A guide for persons who must write a speech for business, political, government, military or public relations purposes. Presents formulas and techniques that show how to write an informative, meaningful, and successful speech, tailored to the speaker's personality. --Only $3.95

S4 - THE EXECUTIVE'S GUIDE TO SUCCESSFUL SPEECHMAKING
by Jack Gren
A practical informative book that shows you how to make a dynamic, interesting speech. Written by one of the nation's leading public speakers, it provides help to busy people everywhere who are asked to speak. --Only $3.50

S5 - MONEY TALKS: The Complete Guide To Creating A Profitable Workshop Or Seminar In Any Field
by Jeffrey Lant, Ph.D.
This is just what you need to turn your expertise into platform gold. Talking is now a multi-billion dollar industry. CHANGING TIMES MAGAZINE says this is the most complete book ever written on how to get into it part-time or full-time. We agree! It's astonishingly complete. 303 pages. --Just $35.00

S6 - NEW LAUGHS FOR SPEAKERS
If you speak in public and need help capturing the attention of your audience, here's a fantastic tool to help you. Hundreds of jokes designed to help the speaker warm up to an audience before, during and after the speech. --Only $5.00

S7- <u>CONVERSATION MADE EASY</u>
 by Elliot Russell

Stimulating conversation is one of life's greatest pleasures, and fortunately the ability to talk convincingly and easily can be learned. This book explains how to overcome shyness, find interesting things to say, tell stories entertaining, and develop a delightful power to converse that will hold the attention of everyone. --Just $5.00

S8 - <u>PRACTICAL GUIDE TO PUBLIC SPEAKING</u>
 by Maurice Forley

Use this book to get off to a quick start! Loaded with workable ideas and easy methods. --Only $5.00

WRITING AND PUBLISHING

W1 - <u>THE BEGINNER'S GUIDE TO WRITING FOR PROFIT</u>
 by Mildred B. Grenier

This book shows how you can write and sell articles, fillers greeting card verses and puzzles. A list of markets where you can sell your writing is included. --Only $3.95

W2 - <u>THE WRITER'S GUIDE TO QUERY LETTERS & COVER LETTERS</u>
 by Gordon Burgett

Query letters are the difference between the amateur and the professional in the writing world. They let you test the market first, know which editor needs your work, focus on the readership, and create a selling article or book every time. This book shows how to write queries that sell, then how to resell that same (or other) work with a cover letter. Thirty examples in total. --Only $12.95

W3 - <u>WRITING AND SELLING INFORMATION THE MAIL ORDER WAY</u>
 by John Riddle

Covers a spare-time business that you can start on a shoestring. This book gives you the "how-to's" of getting started, guides you through selecting, researching and writing your information report, and shows how and where to advertise for best results. Includes a sample report. --Just $3.50

W4 - HOW TO SELL MORE THAN 75% OF YOUR FREELANCE WRITING
by Gordon Burgett

Professionals can't afford to not sell 75% of what they write -nor can you, if articles or nonfiction books are your specialty or dream. In this just updated edition of the landmark text that first revealed the professional's how-to secrets, Burgett tells what highly paid writers do in what order-and how, following the book's step-by-step advice, you can do the same and receive the same rewards!
--Just $12.95

W5 - HOW TO MAKE MONEY WRITING AND SELLING SIMPLE INFORMATION
by Jay Barnes

A priceless collection of workable techniques that will show you the easy steps to turning your knowledge and experience into marketable books and reports that you can sell at 10 times your printing cost or more! You must read this book. --Only $15.00

W6 - HOW TO SELF-PUBLISH YOUR BOOK AND HAVE THE FUN AND EXCITEMENT OF BEING A BEST-SELLING AUTHOR
by Melvin Powers

Melvin knows how to write and/or publish books, and then sell them by the millions! In the arena of self-publishing and mail order books and manual selling, Mr. Powers is a superstar. This book offers the standard self-publishing instructions (how to choose a topic, copyright information, etc.), plus plenty of really creative and insightful advice from a real pro. --Only $20.00

W7 - HOW TO WRITE A HIT SONG AND SELL IT
by Tommy Boyce

This book is what you need when you are serious about writing songs and selling them. Everything you need is right here!
--Just $10.00

W8 - SONGWRITERS RHYMING DICTIONARY
   by Whitfield
This book is ideal for poets as well as songwriters.   --Only $10.00

W9 - HOW TO MAKE YOUR FORTUNE WITH BOOKS
   by Owen Bates and Neal Michaels
Find out what books you can sell--starting small and growing into a full-time operation from your own home. Discover the in's and out's of planning your sales and advertising strategy, testing ad results, mailing list rental, and finding the best sources/dealers to help you sell your books.   --Just $12.00

W10 - HOW YOU CAN MAKE A FORTUNE SELLING INFORMATION BY MAIL: A Step-by-Step Guide To Publishing And Mail Order Profits
   by Russ von Hoelscher
Full time or spare time, the money-making potential of mail order information marketing is tremendous. In this remarkable new book, Russ von Hoelscher, the grand master of mail order and information sales, shows you how to make a fortune in this most rewarding business.   --Only $14.95

TALENT / CAREER

T1 - DISCOVER YOUR TALENT AND FIND FULFILLMENT: A Guide To Using Your Skills To Get What You Need And Want Out Of Life
   by Roscoe Barnes III
This hot, new book is a Talent Primer. It's designed to ignite in you a passion to discover and efficiently use your natural gifts. It aims to help you to find realistic ways to enjoy your dreams.
   --Only $6.95

T2 - TEST YOURSELF - FIND YOUR HIDDEN TALENT
Unsure about what talent you possess? Get this book and find out! Easy, practical, proven methods.   --Just $3.00

T3 - <u>NICHE MARKETING FOR WRITERS, SPEAKERS, AND ENTREPRENEURS</u>: How To Make Yourself Indispensable, Slightly Immortal, And Lifelong Rich In 18 Months!
  by Gordon Burgett
This new book by Gordon is absolutely extraordinary! Read it and become a specialist in your field. Learn how to market yourself--and your knowledge. Everything you need to succeed is between these covers.   --Only $14.95

MODELING

M1 - <u>THE TEENAGER'S GUIDE TO BREAKING INTO TV COMMERCIALS</u>
  by Cortland Jessup
Shows how to determine your "type," how to train at home, how to take and select your best photo, how to get an agent/manager, how to handle an interview and audition plus sample resumes, home practice scripts and a list of agents.   --Only $4.95

M2 - <u>GETTING YOUR BABY INTO MODELING AND TV COMMERCIALS</u>
  by Ray Carlson
This information-packed guide introduces you to the potentially profitable world of baby modeling.   --Only $3.50

M3 - <u>YOU DON'T HAVE TO BE BEAUTIFUL TO BE A MODEL</u>
  by Millkie and Ray Carlson
A beginner's step-by-step guide to the lucrative field of professional modeling.   --Only $3.50

ART: SKETCHING & CARTOONING

SC1 - <u>BIG BUCKS FROM LITTLE SKETCHES</u>: Proven Ways To Earn Money With Portraits And Caricatures Using Little Or No Talent
  by Roscoe Barnes III
Now you can turn a hobby into a thriving money-making venture! Anyone can with the easy methods offered in this hot manual. Students

all over the country are using it to earn extra money. You can too! Cartoon World says, "This is a very good book!" --Just $13.95

SC2 - THE CARTOON COACH: How To Draw Cartoons That Sell!
     by C. Bruce Steffenhagen
Don't even think of becoming a cartoonist until you've studied this book. Get it and learn from a real professional who has over 50 years of successful experience. --Only $14.95

HOW TO ORDER

To order any of these resources, please use the catalog number and/or book title. Order directly from McKinley & Henson, P.O. Box 4382, Gettysburg, PA 17325. Add $2.00 for postage and handling for first order. When you order five or more copies, please add $.50 for each copy, not to exceed $3.00.

ROSCOE BARNES IS AVAILABLE FOR SPEAKING ENGAGEMENTS

Get him to speak at your next meeting!
Roscoe is a dynamic speaker. Write him today! Let him _inspire_..._entertain_...and _inform_ your group on numerous topics.

He's ready now to visit SCHOOLS, CIVIC GROUPS, CHURCHES, YOUTH GROUPS, POLITICAL GROUPS, BUSINESS MEETINGS, and MILITARY AUDIENCES. Among other things, Roscoe will eagerly share on the following subjects:

* Discover Your Talent and Find Fulfillment
* How To Speak with Confidence and Power
* How to Write for Publication and Money
* Professionals: How to Find Fulfillment Within and Beyond the Work-Place
* How to Turbo-charge Your Preaching
* Black History and Martin Luther King Celebrations
* Multi-culturalism
* How to Successfully Promote and Publicize Your Art
* Effective Public Relations for Small Businesses and Non-profit Organizations

Plus a host of other topics on Religion, the Bible, Theology and Church Ministry.

For more information, write:
Roscoe Speaks
P.O. Box 4382
Gettysburg, PA 17325